The Rosary Drama

GW00801660

The Rosary Drama

A Scripture–Based Commentary
and Contemplation

Stephen Redmond SJ

VERITAS

Published 2011 by
Veritas Publications
7–8 Lower Abbey Street
Dublin 1, Ireland
Email publications@veritas.ie
Website www.veritas.ie

ISBN 978 1 84730 269 4
Copyright © Stephen Redmond, 2011

10 9 8 7 6 5 4 3 2 1

A catalogue record for this book is available from the British
Library.

Design by Norma Prause-Brewer, Veritas
Cover design and illustrations by Tanya M. Ross, Veritas
Printed in the Republic of Ireland by Turners Printing Company
Limited, Longford

Veritas books are printed on paper made from the wood pulp of
managed forests. For every tree felled, at least one tree is planted,
thereby renewing natural resources.

DEDICATION

In grateful tribute to my Legion of Mary friends

Contents

Preface

A prayer to celebrate a Mother's joy
the rose, the lovely flower of ecstasy
and so 'rosarium', a rose-ringed lawn
to give the prayer its name

The Light-years: now a man, still Mary's Boy
the teaching, healing, friendship, majesty
and then the Passion-night, the Easter-dawn
the Spirit's wind and flame

A drama surely this, a work of art
a text of Love's achievements, promises
a true-to-life, a hope-filled action-play
whose final act is joy

The Rosary: a prayer of words and heart
dear readers of this book: my prayer is this:
that it may bring you closer day by day
to Mary and her Boy.

ÁTHAS/JOY

Ar theachaireacht an aingil dúbhrais briathar ghrá
is géill tú féin do Ghrá sioraí ó lá go lá
An Chuairt, Magnificat, an Bhreith, an ceol san ngaoith
is Seosamh-díl is Simeon is fir an dlí
A Mhuire, Maighdean-Máthair, 'stú ár ngrá

Announcement and response: be it done to me
the Visit, bringing Christ in courtesy
the Birth, the manger, shepherds, song-filled night
the offering and sword, the nations' light
seeking, finding, home, obedient Son

THE JOYFUL MYSTERIES
The Annunciation
The Visitation
The Nativity
The Presentation
The Finding

The Annunciation

The first two chapters of Luke's gospel (apart from the short prologue) can be described as mainly a meditation on the infancy and childhood of Jesus: a meditation with a focus on his redemptive mission and destiny, a family life 'pre-view' of elements of his public life. Scholars note that the Greek text of the 'meditation' is strongly based on Aramaic, then widely spoken in Palestine, which indicates Aramaic-speaking sources, one of which could well have been Our Lady. Indeed we could say that Luke shaped his text (some of it poetical) largely out of family memories and traditions. I like to think that he wrote the Annunciation text with special reverence.

Gabriel ('hero/strength of God') is presented as 'sent by God': the Christ-Event is a divine initiative. 'Mary' translates the Hebrew-Aramaic 'Miryam', (which perhaps means 'Beloved') and 'Greetings, richly engraced/Hail, full of grace' translates the Greek '*Chaire kecharitómene*'. (Thank you, Luke, for the word-music.) Here we have the first of the many gospel titles of Our Lady. The adjective implies that it is God who favours, engraces: another indication of the divine initiative.

'She was very upset by the greeting and wondered what it could mean': this is the first gospel glimpse of her mind, her feelings. Gabriel reassures her, proclaims the messianic royalty of her child to be, and in regard to her virginity and motherhood attests the absolute sovereignty and power of God and with impeccable angelic courtesy leaves the last word to her.

It is, of course, 'Yes'. Her reply begins with a self-emphasis ('look, I am a servant of the Lord') and ends with a desire, a surrender ('let it be done': in Hebrew-Aramaic idiom, 'let God do it').

In this scene, from the angel's name to the angel's final statement, 'with God nothing will be impossible', and Mary's 'Yes', there is quite a remarkable emphasis on the power of God. God does do it.

Kecharitómene: a lovely word
to set you wondering and fill your heart with spring
Kecharitómene: a lovely chord
angelic melody, a song of things to be
Love came your way and Love came to stay
and night turned to day for all who were yearning for Him
Kecharitómene: a Baby stirred
and so a dream came true, Love came in
thanks to you bringing Him
Chaire Kecharitómene

► *Luke 1:26-38**

**The Scripture reference or references given at the end of each chapter will, it is hoped, encourage the reader to ponder the text or texts on which the chapter is based.*

The Visitation

For part of his infancy narrative, Luke gives parallel accounts of Jesus and John the Baptist. In the Visitation he brings them and their mothers together. This is the most joyful of the joyful mysteries of the Rosary. It is a very human, very 'family', pro-life occasion: the women supporting each other in their welcomed pregnancies, both very aware that the God of life is active in their situations, that their children are children of grace with a destiny altogether special.

Mary set out 'with haste': the Greek phrase can also mean 'very thoughtfully'. Both translations convey her practical charity. 'Elizabeth' is the Greek form of a Hebrew name meaning 'God is fulness' or 'God has sworn (to protect us)'.

'The babe leaped in her womb.' As Luke the physician would have known, an emotional experience of a mother (and Elizabeth was overjoyed by Mary's arrival) can cause a movement of the unborn child. This is probably what happened here. Elizabeth understandably associates her child with her own joy.

'Blessed are you among women and blessed is the fruit of your womb.' Here of course is the source of part of the 'Hail Mary' in which millions beyond numbering have echoed Elizabeth's praise of Our Lady and her Son. 'Fruit of your womb' is a beautiful description of what a child is: a description that challenges the obscenity of abortion. She gives Our Lady three titles: blessed among women, mother of the Lord, she who believed.

Mary's song, called the 'Magnificat' from the first word of the Latin translation, is akin to the Old Testament song of Anna (1 Samuel 2:1-10) but is much more personalised. It can be considered a stylised 'spelling-out' of her 'hand-maid' commitment at the Annunciation. Here she represents all those who humbly, confidently and joyfully celebrate the great deeds of God: the kind of people listed by Jesus in the Beatitudes.

In his encyclical on the Eucharist, Pope John Paul II asked us to consider the Magnificat 'in a Eucharistic key'. Both Song and Eucharist are primarily praise and thanksgiving. 'The Eucharist has been given to us so that our life, like that of Mary, may become completely a Magnificat.'

The most ecumenical prayer of Christians is, of course, the Our Father. Next to it comes the Magnificat. It is in the liturgical evening prayer of the Catholic Church and the Anglican Church and the liturgical morning prayer of the Orthodox Church. Whenever we say or sing it, let us invoke Mary as the mediating Mother of Christian unity.

Two women met in a quiet room
each of them carried a child in her womb
lovely their meeting, lovely their greeting
Spirit-wings beating near

Two women wondered and hoped and prayed
two women lifted their hearts and obeyed
joy beyond telling, happiness welling
Spirit dispelling fear

One of them old, Elizabeth
Mary, the girl from Nazareth
both of them felt the Spirit's breath
presence, delight, perfume

Two women met in desire to give
two women prayed that the world might live
two hearts united, heaven is sighted
there in that quiet room

► *Luke 1:39-50*

The Nativity

'A decree went out from Caesar Augustus that all the world should be enrolled. This was the first enrolment when Quirinius was governor of Syria.' This 'census statement' that introduces Luke's account of the birth of Jesus has been the subject of much scholarly speculation, none of it conclusive. The first-century Jewish historian Josephus says that Quirinius, who became governor of Syria in AD 6, held a census, but this is too late a date for the Lord's birth.

There was an Augustan census in 8 BC and there is some evidence to suggest that Quirinius may have been an important state official ('governor' in a very loose sense) in Syria at that time. Nazareth and Bethlehem were then in the kingdom of Herod the Great, which was not part of the Roman Empire but was dependent on it. It may be that Herod, in a gesture of loyalty, had a supplementary census, or that Rome had taxation rights in his kingdom (a census was a tool of taxation), so that the Augustan census was operative there.

An alternative translation of the Quirinius text ('this census was the one before the one held while Quirinius was governor of Syria') favours the view that the census mentioned by Luke was part of or connected with the general census of 8 BC, which may have lasted into the following year or two. Matthew explicitly and Luke almost explicitly place the birth of Jesus in the reign of Herod, who died in 4 BC.

But enough of census dating. We can take it that Luke is not too worried about exact history here, but is more interested in the paradox of providence that it was through a decree of the political ruler of the immense Roman world that the messianic king of the whole world should be born in Bethlehem. He would doubtless have appreciated (and enjoyed) the irony that the aforementioned political giant had a title, Augustus, of religious connotation.

'Nazareth ... Bethlehem': a distance of about ninety miles. Bethlehem was the home-place of the great king David and the scene of his first royal anointing. A greater king was to be born there with his foster-father of Davidic descent, there to comply with census procedure.

'She gave birth to a son': a basic statement of the Christian faith inviting meditation rather than commentary. 'Her first-born': in biblical Greek this means the child who will continue the family name: it does not necessarily imply other children. 'Swaddling clothes': long strips used to support limbs.

The 'manger', a detail mentioned three times, tells us that Mary and Joseph found shelter in a place for livestock, perhaps part of a hostelry. But it may have been a cave. In the Bethlehem area there were (and are) many caves, and sometimes people built a primitive house in front of a cave, using the cave for their animals. '*Katalyma*', the word used for 'inn' or 'house', can mean a 'guest-room' or 'dining-room', as in Luke 22:12 for the room of the Last Supper.

Having delicately indicated the circumstances of the Birth, Luke, the evangelist of the poor, introduces the very poor: the shepherds. These poor men are enriched with 'the glory of the Lord': a biblical expression conveying the dynamic presence of God. They too have their annunciation, their 'good news' (*evangelion*: gospel). Note how personalised the message is: 'to you is born … a sign for you … you will find a babe …' Jesus is announced in three great titles: Saviour, Christ, Lord. And in his coming the greatness of God is radiantly shown forth ('glory') and for those who accept him all is well ('peace').

As elsewhere, Luke mentions the mind of Mary: here she remembers and ponders. The shepherds, we gather, did not keep their experience to themselves; we could say that the 'good news' of the Saviour-Christ-Lord got its first 'airing' in the sheep-fields of Bethlehem.

Here is the Lord: gather all around
here is the Child that's born to us
come softly, don't make a sound
for he's asleep and his mother is smiling
he will wake later on

Here is the Lord: all his words are true
here is the light of all the world
he brings a message to you
now he's asleep and his mother is waiting
he will speak later on

Here is the Lord: learn to know your friend
here is the kindness of our God
he'll love his own to the end
now he's asleep and his mother is praying
he will die later on

Here is the Lord: just a little boy
here is the glory and the power
he's come to offer you joy
now he's asleep and his mother is singing
he will rise later on

▸ *Luke 2:1-20*

The Presentation

Luke has quite a fondness for scenes in the temple of Jerusalem. A temple scene begins and ends his gospel and quite a few of them occur in his Acts of the Apostles. The temple is the scene of what may be called Jesus' teaching debut at the age of twelve before he returns to the 'hidden life' of Nazareth. And Luke makes the temple the final scene of the encounter between Jesus and the Evil One before he begins his public life. This fondness may indicate the influence of John. In the gospel of John the temple is the scene of much of Jesus' teaching (the Lord confronting the religious establishment on its own ground) and Jesus calls the temple 'my Father's house' and an image of himself in his humanity (John 2:16, 19-21). Here we contemplate Luke's second temple scene: the Presentation.

By Jewish law a mother was 'unclean' for forty days after the birth of a son. This 'uncleanness' was legal and ceremonial (it did not imply any moral fault) and was connected with the awe evoked by the beginning of life as a special showing-forth of divine power. The 'purification' involved two sacrifices: a lamb and pigeon (two pigeons in the case of the poor). The law also required that every first-born male be consecrated or presented to God as special 'divine property' and 'bought back' by a money payment. With some adaptation, Luke combines both rituals with an emphasis on the presentation of the Child as a foreshadowing of the Passion and Death.

He gently highlights the humility and poverty of Mary and Joseph, the humanity of Jesus, the devotedness of Simeon and Anna. Simeon's taking, or rather receiving, the Child in his arms and his blessing Mary and Joseph (a beautiful vignette this) suggests that he was the priest officiating at the presentation ceremony. He foretells Mary's share in the Cross of Jesus, and an acceptance or rejection of Jesus that will reveal what is really happening in the human heart. As evangelist of women, Luke must have been delighted to bring Anna, the elderly temple 'nun' and apostle, into this engraced ensemble.

Simeon's beautiful prayer for peaceful retirement is also a thanksgiving for the coming of Jesus and a prophecy of Jesus' world mission: 'all peoples, glory, light'. It has been in the official night-prayer of the Church for many centuries. It has a special appeal for those who are nearing the end of their earthly days. May they imitate the hope and gratitude of their Jerusalem temple counterparts.

Temple courts astir
Simeon says the Christ has come
bringing light and joy
Nazareth couple, new-born Boy
now I welcome Mary's Son
now I'm young with her

► *Luke 2:22-38*

The Finding

For the second-last sequence in his infancy narrative, Luke brings us back to the temple. Originally, Jewish law required men to attend the feasts of Passover, Pentecost and Tents. But by the time of Christ, those living far from Jerusalem usually attended only Passover. Some rabbis thought that women and children should attend too. 'When he was twelve years old': a Jewish boy officially came of age at thirteen. 'The boy Jesus stayed behind in Jerusalem': he is growing up. 'Jesus' is the only personal name in this sequence. Mary and Joseph are simply 'parents', 'mother', 'father'. Luke is clearly presenting a family situation, but one with a difference.

Their child going missing in a Passover-packed Jerusalem must have been a nightmare for Mary and Joseph. Finding him must have been a tremendous relief. But the dialogue reveals a tension between a very human situation and a more than human mystery.

He is 'sitting' (a posture of authority) among the teachers (rabbis held informal classes in the temple area), listening, answering, creating something of a school sensation: who is this child prodigy from Nazareth? (Is this a pointer towards the debates in Jesus' ministry in John?)

We might respectfully call the Mary of the gospels a woman of few words, but always words demanding attention. Here they are revealingly direct: words implying her and Joseph's authority. Not a word from Joseph; indeed, not a word from him anywhere in the gospels. Jesus' reply concerns a 'father' other than Joseph, a sonship quite beyond the sonship he has with them. This surely is an 'advance notice' of the Father-Son statements in his ministry, especially in John. 'And they did not understand': we can sympathise with them. And then the tension breaks: we can almost see him putting his hands in theirs. And so back to Nazareth.

Is the finding in the temple a foreshadowing of the Resurrection? That it happened on the third day after the losing may be significant. The finding is a re-union with those he loves and who love him. The Resurrection leads to a re-union with those he loves and whom he has formed in love for him and for one another. At the finding he speaks of his Father to Mary and Joseph. On Easter Day he speaks of his Father to Mary Magdalene and his disciples. And surely the Nazareth life that followed the finding was the nearest thing to the risen life a family on earth ever experienced. And one special person was with him throughout: Our Lady of the Finding, of Nazareth, of Easter Day, pray for us.

'Seek and you will find'
so it was with them
the child of Bethlehem
now a maturing boy
a finding full of joy
but fraught with mystery
this Jesus – who is he?
Nazareth days in store
finding him more and more
sharing his heart and mind

▸ *Luke 2:41-52*

Solas/Light

An Baisteach úd ó lámha Eoin – an raibh tú ann?
I bpósadh Cana fíor-miorúilt is gáir is greann
an Ríocht ar fógairt, athrú glórmhar cuirp an Rí
san Eochairist do Mhac mar bia beo ár shlí
a Mhuire, Solas Stiúrtha, 'stú ár ngrá

Jordan: water poured, the humble Lord
Cana: first of signs, the Mother's word
Kingdom, message: come and hear and see
Transfiguration: mountain of majesty
Gift and food and pledge of joy to come

The Luminous Mysteries

The Baptism of Jesus
The Marriage Feast of Cana
The Proclamation of the Kingdom
The Transfiguration of Jesus
The Institution of the Eucharist

The Baptism of Jesus

All the gospels highlight John the Baptist in his ministry of announcing Jesus as the Messiah, the Promised One. That ministry included the conferral of a 'baptism of water' as a token of repentance for sin and of resolve to amend one's life. Mark and Luke briefly mention the baptism of Jesus; John does not mention it at all. But Matthew's account is quite detailed.

He notes Jesus' intention to be baptised. He gives the meeting (which may have been quite sudden) and the conversation between Jesus and John: John's astonishment (the sinless One asking for baptism!) and Jesus' insistence on it being done. He desires to be in his humanity one of those who serve God in radical humility and trust. We have here an anticipation of the beautiful 'Sacred Heart' text of Matthew 11:29: 'Learn from me for I am gentle and lowly in heart.'

The baptism and his 'baptismal mindset' can be seen as the anticipation of his Passion and Death (Jesus speaks later on of his death as a 'baptism'). At the Jordan, as at Calvary, he unites with sinners as their Saviour. Both baptism and Cross invite us to contemplate Jesus in his humanity, in his mission as Saviour.

Matthew, Mark and Luke all record the showing-forth of the Father and Spirit that follows the baptism, with Luke (the evangelist of prayer) noting that Jesus was praying (John mentions only the Spirit). The message here is surely about divine power and love: in biblical usage 'Spirit' denotes power and 'dove' symbolises love; and Jesus is 'the Beloved'.

We are given here a glimpse of Jesus as the gracious and compassionate Servant-Messiah, truly one of us, and also as the unique and majestic Son. There is here what we may call an announcement of the Blessed Trinity, the Trinity that is invoked in the great mandate to preach and baptise given at the very end of Matthew's gospel: the Triune God is integral to both Jesus' baptism and ours. Let us give thanks for this primal sacrament.

John: the voice of prophecy
Jesus: sheer humility
announcement of the Trinity:
God revealed redemptively

▸ *Matthew 3:13-17*
  Mark 1:9-11
  Luke 3:21-22
  John 1:32-34

The Marriage Feast of Cana

There is far more symbolism in John's gospel than in the others; and from 1:19 to 2:11 (immediately after the profound 'Prologue of the Word' in which he proclaims the divinity and humanity of Christ) the evangelist gives us what may be called 'the symbolism of the six-seven days'. He depicts the Lord, the Word made one of us, beginning to bring a new life, a new creation to the world. He arranges a sequence of days in imitation of the 'week' of creation of the world in Genesis, concluding it with a marriage celebration, symbolic of the new intimacy with God through, with and in Christ.

'Cana': the site is uncertain; opinion is divided between Kefr Kenna and Khibert Qana, both near Nazareth.

'The mother of Jesus.' John never calls her by her personal name; he always relates her to Jesus. She appears twice in this gospel: here at the beginning of his ministry, intimately associated with the 'sign' (John's word for certain remarkable deeds of the Lord) of the water-into-wine; and on Calvary at his death, just before the great sign of the blood and water from his side. Given his symbolic approach, it can hardly be doubted that the evangelist is indicating in both scenes her special role in the process of new life in Christ.

A special attraction of the Cana scene is that it has two of the rare gospel sayings of Our Lady. 'They have no wine.' We have here a glimpse of a kindly woman concerned for the new husband and wife and feast-organisers threatened with grave embarrassment. Is it a direct request for a 'sign'? Hard to say. One would love to know the tone of voice, the look on her face. We can safely say that it is Our Lady saying, 'You know what to do'.

'Woman, what have you to do with me? My hour has not yet come.' Again one would love to know the tone of voice, the look on the face. Was he gently teasing her? We should not forget the human side of this intimate interchange. As regards text alone, the reply conveys a certain reserve. In Hebrew-Aramaic idiom, coming from son to mother, 'woman' is very unusual but certainly not disrespectful. It is perhaps close to our formal 'madam'. Here, as at the Cross, it can be plausibly taken as a reminder that he is more than her son and as an indication that she is the 'new Eve'. 'What have you to do with me?' A more literal translation of the original Greek of the gospel (*'ti emoi kai soi'*) is 'what to me and to you?'

'My hour is not yet come.' One interpretation of this text is that the 'hour' refers to the Death-Resurrection as the event that releases and fully manifests his grace and power. It is only because of the Death-Resurrection that Mary's intercession, like every fact of grace, exists and has effect. By the power of Jesus, the Cana 'sign' anticipates the 'hour', is integrated into it in a time-transcending way. Another interpretation sees the text as a rhetorical question ('has not my hour come already?') and 'hour' as referring to the Lord's messianic mission as a whole, with the Cana 'sign' as an early 'moment' of it. And Mary's second Cana saying ('do whatever he tells you' to the servants) is both an act of confidence in her son and a strong indication that a 'sign' is on the way.

The Cana sequence is a delightful blend of realistic detail and human touches with divine power and profound symbolism. 'Signs', 'glory', 'believed': these Cana words are key words in John's gospel as a whole. Here the water-into-best-wine (600 to 700 litres!) is a sign of Jesus as bringer of life and joy in abundance and richness. The 'glory' is of the eternal Word refracted in things of sense. The disciples' faith is not indeed perfect, but rather a seed to be developed through continual contact with Jesus. A headline here for us. And another headline from Mary herself: 'Do whatever he tells you.'

Cana's big day: marriage display
bride and her groom, overpacked room
no more to drink: what will guests think?
Mary's quick word, power of the Lord
waiters fill up cup after cup
Jesus the Guest providing the best

▶ *John 2:1-11*

The Proclamation of the Kingdom

In all four gospels the Lord is presented as a great teacher. In Matthew, Mark and Luke the dominant theme of his teaching is 'the Kingdom', in Matthew, 'of heaven', in Mark and Luke, 'of God'. 'The Kingdom' essentially means the reign and rule of God who is the loving 'Abba' (this being the word used by Aramaic-speaking children in intimate contact with their father). 'Kingdom', of course, implies a community, a people, that is or should be responsive to the 'Abba'.

Much of Jesus' teaching about the Kingdom is in parables. The Greek *'parabole'* literally means 'two-things-alongside-each-other'; that is, two things compared. Comparison is a traditional teaching technique: what the teacher wants to explain is compared to something in the pupils' experience. Jesus' 'Kingdom comparisons' are unequalled in religious literature.

Many of the parables present the God of the Kingdom as merciful and caring (The Errant Son, The Lost Coin, The Lost Sheep), generous (The Great Supper, The Vineyard Owner), responsive to prayer (Caring Parents, The Widow and the Judge, Neighbours at Midnight), welcoming to the humble and critical of the proud (The Tax-Collector and the Pharisee) ...

There are parables that indicate what the People of the Kingdom are like or should be like: seeing the Kingdom as something to be treasured, concerned for the needy, trustful of God, humble, forgiving, commonsensical: The Pearl, The Good Samaritan, Caring Parents, Table Guests, The Wicked Servant, The Tower-Builder ...

The 'nature' parables (The Sower, The Mustard Seed, The Wheat and Weeds, The Yeast ...) point out that the Kingdom is God's doing, God's gift. Parables like The Talents, The Weather Signs, The Rich Fool, The Ten Girls, The Wedding Robe, The Closed Door, The Wicked Vine-Tenders are quite special: they emphasise the Kingdom as a God-given fact that demands urgent attention and response. In them the 'First Citizen' of the Kingdom forcefully challenges and allows no compromise.

Matthew provides a veritable feast of parables. Mark not so: he sees the Kingdom not so much in Jesus' words as in his actions: his Jesus is a dynamic doer. While sharing to some extent with Matthew, Luke has three unforgettable 'parable exclusives': The Errant Son, The Good Samaritan, The Poor Man and the Rich Man. And in his Passion narrative he dramatically relates the Kingdom to Jesus in the immortal death-bed prayer of the crucified thief: 'Remember me when you come into your kingdom.'

The phrase 'kingdom of God' occurs only twice in the gospel of John, in the Jesus-Nicodemus dialogue. There is only one formal parable: that of Jesus the Good Shepherd. But profound (one could say, poetical) comparisons abound: all focusing on the gift of divine life, all Jesus-centred: he is the living bread, the light of the world, the way, the vine, the giver of living water that bubbles into eternal life.

In his Passion narrative John emphasises the royalty and dignity of Jesus: in Gethsemane, in the Jesus-Pilate sequence (here 'king' and 'kingdom' are key words applied to the Lord), in the cry of victory from the Cross ('It is achieved!'), in the lavish anointing of his body. In the Resurrection narrative the royalty is evident: giver of pardon and peace, shepherd, acclaimed as Lord and God, as the Beloved.

The Kingdom of God is still with and in us, indeed in varying degrees in all who explicitly or implicitly accept the values and beliefs that Jesus proclaimed. It is in process towards that momentous 'moment' when it will be completely glorified and at one with its 'First Citizen', in eternal union with him and Father and Spirit.

We link the kingdom with you, dear Lord
in Matthew you're Teacher, rich in word
Emmanuel, Messiah-King
the kingdom's truth is what you bring

in Mark, dynamic, swift in deed
you take a highway that will lead
to Calvary and life beyond
the kingdom's you: do we respond?

In Luke you come as Mary's Boy
you come in mercy, prayer and joy
the poor, the 'little ones' are blessed
the kingdom is their home and rest

In John you are the eternal Word
made one of us: touched, seen and heard
the Father, You and Spirit give
the kingdom of life: in that we live

▸ *Matthew 5:3-10; 6:9-13; 13:1-52; 18:1-7, 10, 23-25; 19:12-30;*
20:1-16; 21:28-43; 22:1-4; 25:1-46
Mark 1:14-15; 10:13-31
Luke 4:14-19; 6:20-26; 11:1-4; 12:29-34; 23:39-43
John 3:3, 5; 18:33-37

The Transfiguration of Jesus

The transfiguration of the Lord is one of the most remarkable episodes of the gospels and is given by Matthew, Mark and Luke in substantially the same terms.

The apostles Peter, James and John see Jesus with face and clothes shining and radiant. (Not long afterwards they will see him in agony, betrayed, arrested in Gethsemane.) Two iconic Old Testament characters, Moses the lawgiver and Elijah the pioneer prophet, join him and converse with him. Peter speaks of making shelters for the majestic trio (echoes here of the Jewish festival of tents commemorating the Egypt-Promised Land trek). There is a cloud (symbol of the presence of God) and a voice saying, 'This is my Beloved Son; listen to him' (in some manuscripts of Luke the title is 'the Chosen One'). And then only Jesus is with them.

The evangelists present the transfiguration as a 'mountain event'. The Bible sees mountains as symbols of divine immensity, power and protection, as places of divine-human communication. There is quite a mention of mountains and high places in the gospels.

In their transfiguration accounts the evangelists differ in one detail or another. Matthew says that Jesus' face shone like the sun and his clothes were luminously white, that the voice terrified the apostles and that Jesus reassured them. Mark, however, does not mention Jesus' face, but says that his clothes had a whiteness not of this world and that Peter spoke incoherently (Luke agrees with him on this).

Luke has the most detailed account with some points exclusive to him. Jesus visited the mountain to pray. He was praying when the change in face and clothes occurred. Moses and Elijah appeared 'in glory' and conversed with Jesus about his forthcoming Jerusalem 'departure' or 'passing'. The apostles saw 'his glory' and were not only overshadowed by the cloud (as in Matthew and Mark) but entered into it. Some scholars hear echoes of John's gospel in Luke's text.

Of the three gospel accounts, Luke's seems to be the most profound, the most helpful to an understanding of the transfiguration. He shows Jesus at prayer. What probably happened was that Jesus' ecstasy of communion with his heavenly Father (and, we might say, with the Holy Spirit) overflowed externally in some way (the face, the clothes) and that the apostles witnessed this ('they saw his glory'), the witnessing being a mystical experience for them, something quite different from any experience they had had of him. What glory did they see? Did they get a glimpse of his sheer divinity, of him precisely as God? Hardly: that would surely have been too much for them. More probably they got a glimpse of him in his glorified humanity, as he would be when risen from the dead (to strengthen and prepare them, so says the traditional view, for their Gethsemane experience). It was a partial glimpse, of course, just as their experience of the Easter Christ would be partial: only in heaven would they have a full experience of the risen Lord.

They were told to 'listen to him', they still had to walk the road of hope – as we are told, as we have to walk. And we are to hope for a fulfilment that includes a bodily transfiguration modelled on his: 'Our true home is heaven,' Saint Paul says in one of the most beautiful of his texts, 'and we are awaiting the coming of our Saviour the Lord Jesus Christ who will transfigure our lowly bodies into likenesses of his own resplendent body' (Philippians 3:20-21).

Transfiguration: a glimpse of Christ in glory soon to be
anticipation: the hope of what we'll be eternally

► *Matthew 17:1-8*
  Mark 9:2-8
  Luke 9:28-36

The Institution of the Eucharist

The momentous event of the institution of the Eucharist is recorded in four passages of Scripture: in the gospels of Matthew, Mark and Luke and in Saint Paul's first letter to the Christians of Corinth.

The earliest text is Paul's, dating back to about thirty years after the event: 'I received from the Lord what I passed on to you, that the Lord Jesus on the night of his betrayal took some bread and, having given thanks, he said, "This is my body that is for you. Do this in memory of me." In the same way, after supper, he took the cup and said, "This cup is the new covenant in my blood. Do this, every time that you drink it, in memory of me."'

Luke's text varies in early sources but the mainstream manuscript tradition strongly favours a text which is almost identical with Paul's and has the 'body' 'given for you' and the 'cup' 'poured out for you'. The Matthew and Mark texts are similarly twinned, with Matthew adding 'for the forgiveness of sins' to the words over the cup.

The Scripture record is of a new mode of Christ's presence; of a sacrifice which as regards priest and what is offered is identical with Calvary but in its mode of offering is new and to be continued ('given, poured out, do this in memory of me'): of a new nourishment ('eat, drink'); of a new relationship with God ('new covenant').

The reality that Christ instituted in the Supper Room is of stupendous importance in the Christ-Event, indeed, in the ongoing event of the human race. It is, of course, a Reality of Love. Catholic teaching echoes the Scripture record uncompromisingly, encouragingly, appealingly. On that night of betrayal the Lord made himself present in his objective reality under the external forms ('the appearances') of bread and wine, this involving the change whereby the basic reality that makes bread to be bread and wine to be wine ('the substance') became by divine power the reality of his body and blood. He offered himself under these 'appearances' in sacrifice to his heavenly Father. By the words 'do this in memory of me' he established the apostles as priests so that through them and their successors in the priesthood Christians might have him in the Eucharist as their sacrifice and nourishment on their pilgrim way into eternal life and joy.

The gospel of John has the Lord in the bread of life discourse presenting himself as the Eucharistic pledge of eternal life. In its Last Supper sequence, while not recording the institution of the Eucharist, it has him speaking at length of union with him and the Father and Spirit. It also shows him washing the apostles' feet to remind them (and us) that loving outreach towards others is an essential part of a Eucharist-centred life.

The conclusion of Pope John Paul's encyclical on the Eucharist, the last and most personalised of his encyclicals, comes to mind: 'In the Eucharist Christ walks with us ... and enables us to become for everyone witnesses of hope.'

I am God provident
I give a sacrament
the Body and Blood of Christ
the God-Man sacrificed
the bread of life, of heaven
my people's nourishment
all this given

The sea is in the fish
the fish is in the sea
so in the Eucharist
I in you, you in Me
the Love that will not cease
the Ocean of peace
(adapted from the Dialogue of St Catherine of Siena)

▸ *Matthew 26:26-28*
Mark 14:22-24
Luke 22:19-20
I Corinthians 11:23-25
John 6:51-58; 13:3-11

BRÓN/SORROW

Id' chroí an pian: Gethsemane, an lasc gan trua
na dealga, an scigereacht, an bóthar crua
i dtaoibh na Croise seasann tú chomh lán de bhrón
ag glacadh clainne, Máthair dúinne, Máthair Eoin
A Mhuire, Bean na hAoine, 'stú ár ngrá

The moon on Kedron, agony within
behold the Man: the rip of whip on skin
thorns into head, the robe, the reed, the jeers
cross carried, Cyrenean, women's tears
the death, the open Heart, the deed is done

THE SORROWFUL MYSTERIES

The Agony in the Garden
The Scourging
The Crowning with Thorns
The Carrying of the Cross
The Crucifixion and Death

The Agony in the Garden

After the Last Supper Jesus and his disciples went to a place familiar to them just outside Jerusalem. Luke says that it was Mount Olivet. The other evangelists are more specific: John shows them crossing the valley of the Kedron (a seasonal water-course) and entering a garden; Matthew and Mark, while mentioning Mount Olivet, show them coming to a place called Gethsemane ('olive alley, olive press'). Here, according to the traditional view, the Passion began – though it could be argued that it began with the departure of Judas from the Supper Room on his mission of betrayal.

All the gospel accounts of the scene are detailed and dramatic. Those of Matthew and Mark are almost identical. They show Jesus choosing Peter, James and John as his companions in his ordeal and finding them disappointingly unhelpful, with his words to his Father and to them starkly revealing his humanity.

Mark has two 'exclusives': the young man escaping into the night who may well have been himself; and the precious and poignant detail that Jesus called his Father 'Abba', an Aramaic word of confidence, affection and intimacy. The word quickly entered Christian prayers (see Romans 8:15 and Galatians 4:6): a lesson here for us.

Luke's Gethsemane account has much in common with that of Matthew and Mark, but, as in his gospel generally, he has his own approach: he simply says 'disciples' (no names, no number); that Jesus prayed 'about a stone's throw' from where they were; that Jesus healed the cut-off ear of the high priest's servant (a detail interesting to a physician); and in a text not found in all early manuscripts of his gospel he says that an angel came to support Jesus and (another medically interesting point) that his sweat was like drops of blood. Only Luke calls Jesus' ordeal an *'agonia'*.

The harrowing climax of the garden of Gethsemane sequence is the Judas kiss. Matthew and Mark record it. Luke mentions Judas' intention but not the action itself. John's emphasis in his gospel on the dignity of the Lord is evident in his depiction of him in Gethsemane: no agony, not a word about a kiss, Judas just standing there (not called 'one of the Twelve' as he is by Matthew, Mark and Luke), Jesus' words to his captors quite different to those given by the other evangelists with 'I am he' (echoing the 'I am' texts elsewhere in John's gospel) said three times. To sum up: Jesus in command – the King.

The Gethsemane scene is unforgettable to believers in the Lord. As given by Matthew, Mark and Luke, it graphically reveals how genuinely he shared our nature: here is a man in deep trauma and turmoil, asking, as he had never asked before, for human support in a crisis. Let our Gethsemane prayer be a watching with him. But let us also remember, as John did, that he is always the King.

Kedron, you're more than just a brook
you've played your part in God's own book
you've seen the prophets and the kings
you've heard the song the Spirit sings

Put on the glory of the moon
and sing your most adoring tune
tonight the Lord is passing by
tomorrow he will go to die

You'll see him flat in agony
you'll hear him say, 'please watch with me'
you'll hear his Abba-Father prayer
kiss and arrest – all this you'll share

Kedron, personified in verse
in fact a seasonal water-course
hallowed by Him of Nazareth
who crossed it on his way to death

▸ *Matthew 26:36-56*
  Mark 14:32-52
  Luke 22:39-53
  John 18:1-12

The Scourging

Scourging was part of the Roman penal code in Jesus' time: the *'flagellatio'* done with a leather last reinforced with pieces of bone or metal and the less severe *'verberatio'* done with rods. (Scourging was also in the Jewish code: in Jesus' time it was limited to thirty-nine strokes to ensure that the Deuteronomy rule of forty strokes was kept.) Roman scourging was inflicted on slaves and on those socially free but not on Roman citizens, as Saint Paul strongly pointed out when so threatened (Acts of the Apostles 22:25-28).

Jesus was subjected to the 'horrible punishment', as Latin authors called it, of the *'flagellatio'*. It was often used as a prelude to crucifixion and was often lethal itself. Matthew, Mark and John mention the scourging but do not describe it. Luke quotes Pilate as intending to have Jesus so dealt with but does not give the actual event. Matthew and Mark present the scourging as a prelude to the crucifixion. In John and more clearly in Luke (whose 'Pilate passage' here is quite detailed) it is presented as Pilate's substitute for the cross, as the harassed governor's compromise solution to a situation that is becoming more urgent by the minute.

In Gethsemane the suffering is of the soul, of 'the spirit'. Here the emphasis is on the body: the body fully developed from that given him by Mary and the Spirit, the instrument of so much good done to others, the medium of so much human interchange, the reality 'heard and seen and touched' (1 John 1:1), now mercilessly maltreated and horribly wounded. We may be allowed to think that in this harrowing phase of his Passion, Jesus united himself in love with all those (past, present and future in time to him) similarly sinned against, including so many contemporaries of our own. Let us pray accordingly.

A very special Body this:
the fruit of God's own promises
of Mary and divinity
something to touch and hear and see
a proof that he has come to dwell
among us, our Emmanuel
love-medium, uniquely graced
now mutilated, torn, defaced
and Christ who came that all might live
prays for the scourgers, 'Father, forgive'

▸ *Matthew 27:26*
 Mark 15:15
 Luke 23:22
 John 19:1

The Crowning with Thorns

When Jesus was brought before the Sanhedrin, the supreme religious court of the nation, the charge was blasphemy. To get Pilate interested, the charge was made political: he was subverting the nation, claiming to be a king in opposition to Caesar whom Pilate represented. The expression 'king of the Jews' was bandied about and picked up by the soldiers garrisoning Pilate's headquarters. It is probable they were not regular army personnel; more likely Syrian mercenaries supplied by Pilate's immediate superior, the imperial legate of Syria. Perhaps from boredom, some of them made Jesus the butt of a 'meet the king' game. They probably got the thorns from their supply of firewood and probably modelled the crown on the 'sun-ray' crown worn by the Hellenised kings of the Near East.

In his scourging, Jesus shared the pain of many condemned to crucifixion. In the 'meet the king' game he is the sole target, the sole victim. Matthew's and Mark's identical accounts of the appalling scene are quite detailed, John's less so. Luke does not mention the episode at all.

This 'King' section of John's Passion narrative (18:33-39; 19:2-22) is, we can say, a drama within a drama with its varied characters and dialogue: the prisoner speaking of his other-world kingdom and his mission of truth; the soldiers and their pseudo-salute; the cornered and compromising and perplexed Pilate wondering about truth, placarding Jesus as the 'Nazarene King of the Jews' and exiting with his 'what I have written, I have written'; the religious establishment and its supporters with their threatening ultimatum to Pilate and their relentless 'Crucify!' chant.

We contemplate what Jesus said and renew our loyalty to him. We contemplate what the soldiers did and pray for those who reject Jesus through ignorance or insensitivity or even sheer hatred. We contemplate what Pilate said and wrote and pray for those who even confusedly seek the truth.

'King of kings and Lord of lords'
so Handelians sing 'Messiah'
but here no concert hall, no choir
but mocking acts and ribald words
a soldiers' game to pass the time
their Good Friday pantomime
'we'll have our fun, we'll have our jibe
not just at him but all his tribe'

And Christ who came that all might live
prays for the gamesters, 'Father, forgive'

▸ *Matthew 27:27-31*
  Mark 15:16-20
  John 18:33-39; 19:2-22

The Carrying of the Cross

Crucifixion was frequent in the Roman world as a punishment for those convicted of crimes like murder and treason. Roman citizens were not subjected to it. It was usual for the condemned man to carry, not the complete cross, but the crossbeam to the place of execution where, as a rule, the vertical beam was a permanent fixture. A placard around his neck displayed his name and his crime.

We can reasonably suppose that Jesus was so placarded on his way to Calvary. All the evangelists mention the inscription above his head on the cross but only John gives the full wording: 'Jesus the Nazarene King of the Jews'. It expressed Pilate's savage and insulting irony directed against Jesus' enemies. And despite their protest he stood by it in his final (and splendid) exit-line in the gospel drama: 'What I have written I have written.'

John says that Jesus carried his cross. Matthew, Mark and Luke tell us that Simon of Cyrene (in present-day Libya), presumably a pilgrim in Jerusalem for the Passover, was commandeered into cross-carrying service; Luke shows him shouldering the cross behind Jesus. Whether he took over the crossbeam or shared it with Jesus is not entirely clear. Mark says that he was the father of Alexander and Rufus, who were probably with Mark in the same local church and therefore among the first recipients of his gospel.

Luke, the evangelist who highlights the place of women in the life of the Lord, records the encounter between him and 'the daughters of Jerusalem'. Here we have his last prophetic utterance before death and a reminder that there was some compassion along the way to Calvary.

The Stations of the Cross, dating back to the medieval crusades to the Holy Land, have added to this phase of the Passion: the three falls, the Veronica moment and, most of all, the meeting of Mother and Son (beautifully presented in the film *The Passion of the Christ*). They have enriched the devotion of Christians beyond numbering to the One who suffered. It is good to have them in or near churches where the One who suffered and is now risen is still priest, sacrifice, nourishment and presence.

This last part of his Passion walk (and there had been so much walking) was where Jesus was joined by his two fellow prisoners carrying their crossbeams and placards. Let us not forget them in our contemplation. He was to promise paradise to one of them. The other – who knows? He loved them both. Nor let us forget Simon and the lamenting women: Passion prototypes, we could say, of the helping hand and understanding heart.

The praetorium to Calvary procession was probably straggly enough with the chief participants tortured and rejected and, in the eyes of 'the world', losers without hope. There have been so many such processions in the history of our wounded world. But Christians contemplating that Good Friday scene can see in it the promise of another kind of procession: a human pilgrimage, often straggly and difficult, but engraced with hope and led by One who endured the Cross and entered into joy (Luke 24:26; Hebrews 12:2).

Procession starts: no pomp or circumstance
no gilded chariot, no trumpet call
occasional fall, agonised advance
three men cross-beamed, one of them in his heart
carries the wounded world to be redeemed
and rescued by the giving of himself

So it still is: we're on our pilgrimage
we struggle, fall, get up, regain our way
Jesus is still the Sacrament of Help
at every stage, into eternal day

▸ *Matthew 27:32*
 Mark 15:21
 Luke 22:26-31
 John 19:17

The Crucifixion and Death

The evangelists do not give the gruesome procedure to which the Lord was almost certainly subjected: being stretched on the ground, the arms affixed to the crossbeam, being hoisted to the vertical beam, to which the feet were affixed, the fastening of both arms and feet done by either ropes or nails, with the nails reinforced by ropes to keep the body in place. (That Jesus was nailed emerges from the 'group scene' in Luke 24 and the 'Thomas event' in John 20.) But they do go into considerable detail about the ensuing hours on Calvary. Here we focus, as they did, almost entirely on Jesus himself.

The accounts of Matthew and Mark are almost identical. They both give the same 'word' from the Cross: Jesus' cry of desolation: 'My God, my God, why hast thou forsaken me?', the beginning of Psalm 21/22 – no 'Abba' here. They both have the centurion acknowledging Jesus as 'a son of God', but Mark has an exclusive tableau: this officer in charge of the execution, on the alert, 'who stood facing him'.

Luke has three 'words', all of them exclusive to his gospel: Jesus asking his Father to forgive; Jesus commending himself before he dies to his Father; and the absolutely unforgettable promise of paradise to the crucified thief beside him (of which Chesterton said in his famous *The Everlasting Man*, 'Is there anything to put after that but a full stop?').

John has his three exclusive 'words': Jesus entrusting his mother and his beloved disciple to each other: a very human 'family' act of caring but also seen as an entrusting of his people to her in a unique relationship of grace; 'I thirst': understood by the bystanders as a plea for bodily relief but, as with the previous 'word', surely bearing a deeper meaning; 'It is done, finished, achieved': a royal cry of victory. And so the King dies. And John completes his contemplation of Jesus crucified with the post-death revelation of the water and blood, symbolic of utter giving, utter love.

Almost too much to contemplate here, we might think. But contemplate we must if we really want to say with Saint Paul, 'I live by faith in the Son of God who loved me and gave himself for me' (Gal 2:20).

Molaimis go léir an tAon Mhac Críost
do cheannaigh go daor ar an gcrois chéasta sinn ...
'Sé duirt an Rí glan Críost gan cháim
'Ó féach go cruinn ar mo chroí is ar mo chneáibh'
is léir gur sinn d'fhulaing pianta's páis ...
míle buíochas leat, a Aon Mhic mhín
do céasadh, a Rí is naofa dlí ...
(*Paidir traidisiúnta*)

Let us all praise the Christ, the only Son
In costly death that we might live in him ...
Listen to his words on Calvary
'gaze upon my heart, upon my wounds'
for us he bore the cross, the suffering ...
a thousand thanks to you, dear Saviour-King
for dying with a love that knew no bounds
(*Traditional Prayer*)

► *Matthew 27:33-50*
Mark 15:22-39
Luke 23:33-47
John 19:17-34

GLÓIR/GLORY

An t-É a rug tú, féach anois, fíor-Aiseirí
an Deascabháil: do chuir tú slán le Mhac do chroí
an Spiorad Naomh a thánaig chugat, anseo arís
an Deastógáil is Coronú is glóir is fís
a Mhuire, Banríon neimhe, 'stú ár ngrá

Deed done indeed: Risen! deathless Word
Victor coming home, trail-blazing Lord
Spirit: fire and wind to change the earth
Mother called to joy: new Nazareth
Handmaid crowned by Love, the Three, the One

THE GLORIOUS MYSTERIES

The Resurrection
The Ascension
The Coming of the Holy Spirit
The Taking of Our Lady into Heaven: The Assumption
The Crowning

The Resurrection

The gospels do not narrate the actual resurrection itself but they do narrate the discovery of the empty tomb and the appearances of the risen Lord to his friends, both men and women. In Matthew, Mark and Luke the announcement of the resurrection and the first appearance are to women, in John to one woman: Mary Magdalene. There is no gospel mention of an appearance to Our Lady. Perhaps the gospel makers considered that a mere mention would be disrespectful and an account intrusive. (St Ignatius Loyola, with strong feelings on the subject, includes such a meeting in his *Spiritual Exercises*.) Saint Paul introduces his famous piece on the resurrection of the dead with a list of appearances of the risen Lord, including one to 'over five hundred of our brothers'.

In these appearances to his friends, Jesus identifies himself as the Jesus they had known, though in his humanity he has begun a new phase of life. His body, still wound-scarred, is the body in which he had suffered and died but now it has a new perfection, it is free from suffering and death, from the limitations of space and time. And his psyche is free from the fear and anxiety he had experienced at certain points in his pre-resurrection life. He is giving his friends an experience of himself in his glorified humanity: a partial experience without even the radiance of the transfiguration: a complete awareness of the risen Lord will be theirs only in heaven. In all this he is (as Saint Paul was to emphasise) the model, the prototype of the resurrection of all those who die 'in Him', the exemplar of the new life offered to the human race.

In these appearances as recorded in the gospels, he is very much the Lord, the Friend: teaching, encouraging, forgiving, commanding, definitively instituting the sacrament of penance in the Church, making Peter its chief steward, promising to be permanently present in it. All the appearances invite contemplation.

Five of them may be specially mentioned: in Luke the Emmaus episode, deeply symbolic of the presence of Jesus as the Lord of hope; in John the personalised one-to-one encounter with Thomas, the meeting with Mary Magdalen (also personalised and one-to-one) in the lyrical setting of a garden at dawn, the breakfast meeting with the disciples on a dawn-lit lake-shore, symbolic of Jesus as the Bread of the Church; in Matthew the mountain meeting with Jesus mandating a world-mission for the Church with himself as its Emmanuel: God with us. In the Thomas scene Jesus blesses all those who have not seen but still believe (the only beatitude in John). At this point, as it were, the disciples step back and we come in.

He came like a boy at the start of a holiday
he came with a joy that was loveliness all the way
he came as a friend to console them and set them free
a love without end in a radiant company
He came in splendour, tender and strong
no more of crying, dying, now life's the song
he came like a bird that is singing to greet the dawn
he came with a word that keeps echoing on and on
he came like a man to the one who has all his love
he hurried, he ran to the friends he was thinking of
he said, 'I'm living, giving, coming to stay'
he came like a boy on holiday

▸ *Matthew 28:1-10, 16-20*
 Mark 16:1-18
 Luke 24:1-49
 John 20:1-29, 21:1-22
 Paul 1 Corinthians 15:3-57
 Philippians 3:20-21

The Ascension

When Jesus 'rose again on the third day', as we say in the Creed, it did not simply mean a return to the kind of life that he was leading before. Death and suffering have no more power over him. A new freedom, a new glory, a new power is manifest. In his humanity he has begun his 'eternal Sunday', 'he has entered into his rest', as the epistle to the Hebrews says. He is more fully 'with the Father', quite clearly 'the Lord', belonging to a world that is divine.

But for a time he maintains sense-contact with the world as we know it. He appears to his friends to impress on them the glorious reality of himself and to prepare them for their mission of witnessing to him. But after 'forty days' (we need not take the number literally: it means a more or less prolonged period) there is a definitive withdrawal of his palpable visible presence from 'our' world into what we call 'heaven'. This is what we term the 'Ascension'.

We should not think of the Ascension as an isolated event. It is part of a 'glory continuum' of Christ in his humanity that began with the resurrection or (according to John) with the Passion. Saint Thomas Aquinas gives as a reason for his withdrawal that 'our' world was not a good enough setting for him in his glorified state.

Mark describes the Ascension as the taking into heaven of 'the Lord Jesus'. Luke mentions it both in his gospel and his Acts of the Apostles and places it in the Bethany/Mount Olivet area. He gives the beautiful detail that Jesus departed from his disciples with hands uplifted in blessing. This sums up his priestly relationship in his humanity with them and all believers in him.

The epistle to the Hebrews celebrates the heavenly high-priesthood of Jesus: 'he is the mediator of a new covenant ... in the presence of God on our behalf ... he holds his priesthood permanently ... he always lives to make intercession'. That priesthood is operative on earth, especially in the matter of forgiveness of sins which he emphasised in his 'forty days' of risen life and most especially in the Eucharist which he instituted on the eve of his Passion: operative, that is, until he comes again 'to save those who are eagerly waiting for him' (Hebrews 7:24, 25; 9:15, 24, 28).

Some early manuscripts of Luke add that 'he was carried up into heaven'. The Greek verb is *'anephereto'*, used elsewhere in Scripture to denote the offering or immolation of a sacrifice. Christ in his humanity 'goes' to the Father as a Gift that has been offered and accepted. And let us remember that he 'ascends' as our trail-blazer, path-finder, head. Pope Saint Leo the Great says in a famous sermon: 'Human nature ascends ... and shares the throne of the Father. Christ's ascension is our advancement: where the head has gone before in glory, there the body is called in hope.' This is advancement indeed. This is what Christian humanism involves and leads to. Let us praise and rejoice in our liturgies and rosaries and hearts and lives.

Victorious over sin he comes
and shows his Father with delight
the glory of that human-ness
in which he won his fight

Dear Christ, our Saviour, Lord of life
we thank you for the hope you've given
in you our nature, what we are
has reached the heart of heaven

So we on earth are one in joy
with heavenly friends, angelic powers
though gone to them, you're in our hearts
you're with us, of us, ours!
(from the Office of Ascension)

▸ *Luke 24:50-51*
  Acts of the Apostles 1:9-11
  Mark 16:19

The Coming of the Holy Spirit

In a remarkable scene in John's gospel, Jesus proclaims himself the source and giver of 'living water'. The evangelist comments that Jesus was referring to the Spirit that believers would receive when Jesus was glorified. This is the Spirit whom Jesus mentions so profoundly in the same gospel in his Last Supper discourse: the indwelling Holy Spirit of truth, the teacher, the enlightener, the *'paracletos'* (literally, one called to your side, a helper, a friend when you are in need). In John's resurrection narrative, Jesus communicates this Spirit to some of his friends in regard to the sacrament of penance.

In the Acts of the Apostles, Luke describes a spectacular coming of the Spirit to a company of believers which surely included Our Lady. It happens at Pentecost, a Jewish harvest festival. This particular Pentecost becomes what can be called the public inauguration of the Church, the beginning of a vast spiritual harvest.

The power of the Spirit is dramatically externalised in two great forces of nature, wind and fire, and in the disciples' ecstatic acknowledgement of the deeds of God. In his graphic discourse, the first sermon in the history of the Church, Peter presents the death and resurrection of Jesus and the coming of the Spirit as the basic Good News with its promise of forgiveness and new life. His 'international' congregation is prophetic of the world mission of the Church.

By the time of Christ, Pentecost, as well as being a harvest festival, may have become a celebration of law from God and covenant with God. The Spirit-powered Pentecost may have been seen by the first Christians as the divine confirmation of the new law and new covenant derived from Christ.

The influence of the Spirit in that particular Pentecost can also be seen in Luke's picture of the infant Church just after the event: praying, sharing, rejoicing, reverencing, giving thanks, witnessing by example. As we can do too.

An Spiorad Naomh umainn
ionainn agus againn
an Spiorad Naomh cughainn
bíodh, a Chríost, go hobann
(*Maol Íosa Ó Brolcháin*)

Dear Christ, may the Spirit
come swiftly to meet us
surround us, be with us and in us

► *John 7:37-39; 14:16-18; 15:26; 16:13-15; 20:19-23
Acts of the Apostles 2:1-47*

The Taking of Our Lady into Heaven: The Assumption

'The Immaculate Mother of God, the ever-Virgin Mary, having completed the course of her earthly life, was assumed body and soul into heavenly glory.' These are the key words in Pope Pius XII's proclamation in 1950 of Our Lady's being taken in her full reality of body and soul into heaven as a dogma of the Catholic faith, as a divinely revealed part of the Christ-Event. It is a 'companion dogma' to that of the Immaculate Conception, proclaimed in 1854 by Pope Pius IX: one dogma relating to the beginning of her natural life, the other to its ending.

Scripture does not explicitly mention this Taking, but there are texts that provide a pattern of convergence, prophecy, appropriateness and symbolism concerning it. In his Annunciation and Visitation scenes, Luke has Gabriel and Elizabeth greeting Our Lady in unique terms of honour. John, the evangelist of signs and double-meaning, records her intervention and influence at Cana, and her presence and Jesus' 'word' to her and the beloved disciple at the Cross, pointing in both scenes to a redemptive and 'new life' intimacy between her and her Son. In the Book of Revelation, the author, probably with Our Lady in mind, personifies the Church victorious over evil as a woman of cosmic majesty. And two texts in the Adam and Eve sequence in Genesis may contain a prophetic hint or nuance of Mary as the 'new Eve'.

In the early Church Our Lady was championed as the 'new Eve' by Saint Justin, lay apologist and martyr, and Saint Irenaeus, defender of the humanity of Jesus and of the goodness of God's creation (both of them, we may note, only a few generations in time after her). The concept entered popular, or at least monastic, devotion: a medieval hymn in her honour makes a wordplay of it: 'accepting Gabriel's "Ave"/and thus reversing "Eva"/establish us in peace'. Pope Pius XII emphasises the concept in his dogma statement.

Her life was closely modelled on that of her Son in his humanity: in her utter obedience to the divine will, in holiness, in suffering and joy. No human person was as united to him as she was. The Taking into heaven was the culmination of that union. It was an event modelled on his resurrection-ascension, involving her full reality, body and soul. And it happened 'now': God, as it were, in a hurry to have the Mother of the Word-made-one-of-us complete and glorious in heaven: the divine initiative, we could say, delightfully and swiftly operative.

Seeing the Three, the One
re-union with your Son
heaven at last – and yet
earth-things you can't forget:
Nazareth, Calvary
your pilgrim family
Mother, lovely, alive
ensure that we arrive

▶ *Genesis 3:15; 3:20*
  Luke 1:42-43
  John 2:3, 5, 9
  Revelation 12:1

The Crowning

The Taking of Our Lady into heaven is God's definitive welcome of her in her full reality into the eternally experienced Presence, a 'placing' of her 'on the edge of the Trinity' – *'ar theorainn na Trínóide'*, as traditional Celtic devotion beautifully and graphically enshrined her. In our limited human way and in keeping with human tradition and protocol, we envisage a 'ceremonial sequel' to the Taking, a divine affirmation of her unique dignity, of her unique relationship with Christ who has 'all authority in heaven and on earth' and with his people: the Crowning.

The messiah announced to Our Lady in the gospel of Luke is certainly royal: he will be divinely enthroned and his kingdom will last forever. We can reasonably infer that the messiah's mother is royal too. And this is said of her in the Visitation scene: Elizabeth is overwhelmed that 'the mother of my Lord' should visit her. In Aramaic or Hebrew (one of these languages was Elizabeth's vernacular) 'mother of the Lord' meant 'queen-mother'. There may be a hint of royalty in Mary's Song, the Magnificat, that includes a statement of her status-in-Christ: 'He who is mighty has done great things for me. All generations will call me blessed.' Royalty has been described as 'the right to command'. The first miracle of Christ's ministry is prefaced by a word of command from his mother: 'Do whatever he tells you.' And the crowned woman of Revelation 12:1, protected by God, may be a presentation of her as well as of the Church.

Mary has a unique but, of course, subordinate share in the royal rule of Christ. Her queenship has to do with grace: the actual sharing in God's life and the impetus towards sharing in it and growing in it. It is a gift both for her and us, a beautiful element of the Christ-Event. It is a ministry of mercy, of intercession, of sheer love. It reflects in a heavenly way her femininity, her delicate understanding, her sense of one-to-one.

And it is a reality of special power. She is the 'Virgin (and Mother) most powerful', expressed, as I recall, in the wonderful strong-faced statue of her at Ballintubber, Co. Mayo, holding the Child, not at her breast but high up as if in challenge, as if to say, 'This is the One who matters, the One you need'. And her command still is, 'Do whatever he tells you'.

Mary is crowned by royal decree
thanks for this heavenly liturgy
this giving, sharing, mirroring
of rule of love by heaven's King
the ever-blessed Trinity

Mary is crowned: her diadem
a symbol of hope for us from Them
reminding us of what's in store:
royal joy forevermore
praise the Lord! Amen! Amen!

▸ *Luke 1:32-33, 43, 49, 52*
John 2:5
Revelation 12:1